THIS CAT
DOES NOT LOVE YOU

STRIPES PUBLISHING
An imprint of the Little Tiger Group
1 The Coda Centre, 189 Munster Road,
London SW6 6AW

First published in Great Britain in 2017

Text copyright © Emma Young, 2017
Illustrations copyright © Katie Abey, 2017

ISBN: 978-1-84715-805-5

The right of Emma Young and Katie Abey to be identified as the
author and illustrator of this work respectively has been asserted by them
in accordance with the Copyright, Designs and Patents Act, 1988.

A CIP catalogue record for this book is available from
the British Library.

Printed and bound in China.
STP/1800/0135/0217
10 9 8 7 6 5 4 3 2 1

THIS CAT
DOES NOT LOVE YOU

EMMA YOUNG & KATIE ABEY

Hi.

You humans don't actually know anything about cats, do you?

I've lived with my human for five years, and I still end up repeating myself over and over again.

This is what I would tell her if she could speak Cat.

Er... There's only one cat
around here.

Hint: me.

Why leave stuff lying around if you
don't want me to sleep on it?
I'm not a mind reader.

You're not the only one who needs a holiday.

Why would I willingly climb
inside a plastic box if it results in a
thermometer up my bottom?

I've just had that nightmare again about being chased by a gang of giant cucumbers...

There's always room for a little one.

Why, when you see me asleep, do you feel the need to pick me up?

There's something very suspicious
about this wall.

I'm keeping an eye on it but maybe
we should call the police?

I worked out long ago that there wasn't any milk coming out of your top but let me have my fun, okay?

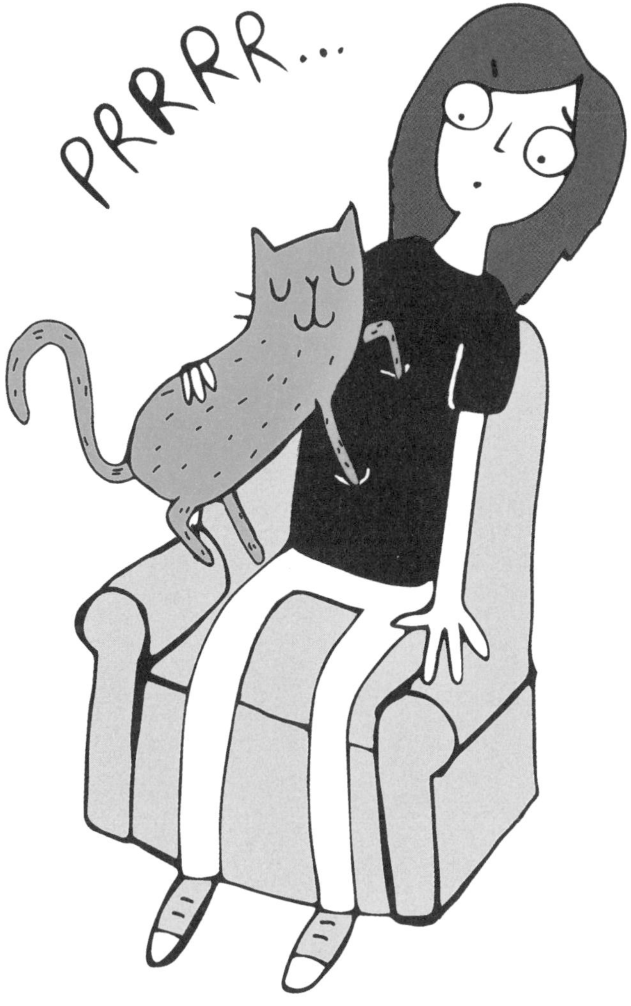
PRRRR...

Whoops.

Well don't blame me – you should
put your stuff away.

I mean, would it kill you to give
me some privacy?

Keep that foul-smelling poison
away from me.

Anyway, what's all the fuss? I don't mind hosting a few friends now and then – get used to it.

Soooo warm and toasty...

Why must you keep poking me?

Seriously.

What fresh hell is this?

Hello? Hello? Hello? Hello? *Hello?*

Welcome to my evil lair.

Camouflage *and* central heating – perfect.

Not bad.

Think I preferred the salt and
vinegar we had last week.

Listen, stupid, I'm trying to help.

This big woolly thing was about to
attack you and you're not even
trying to stab it with the
sharp pointy things.

You're not the only one who likes
a lazy Sunday morning
with the papers...

You missed a bit.

You're not the *worst* owner
in the world.

This scratching post was a
thoughtful gift and it was generous
of you to get me four of them.

Finally, some suitable accommodation.

Seriously? I'm like a hundred times cuter than Mr February.

I don't understand.

You make this lovely warm bed
for me then you immediately
turf me off it.

What kind of a person are you?

Morning madam, this is your
5 a.m. wake-up call.

You're welcome.

No rush, I'm just admiring the view.

That's good quality fur, that.

It might be worth something
on Ebay?

I would rescue you from that
horrendous noisy beast but I've …
er … got somewhere to be.

This muck again? I ordered
Lobster Thermidor!

Sorry to interrupt, but I just pooed
in the bath.

How did they get in here?

I told you we should have got a
microchip cat flap!

This isn't bad, but next time can you buy me one with more flavour?
It's kind of bland.

Let me out.

Let me in.

Let me out.

Let me in.

Keep up, will you!

Ah, there you are...
Just checking.

Why did you put the best one
at the top?

That's just cruel, especially in the
season of goodwill.

I love paper more than Uncle Ted
will love his present. Fact.

I've been sitting on them for six weeks and you haven't noticed.

Why don't you go and watch another boxset?

Cats need fifteen hours sleep a day.
Have some respect for my
body clock.

Hello, RSPCA?

In human years I'm 72 – whatever happened to respecting your elders?

So, I wanted to discuss my food.
Surely you can afford the one that
has parsley on it in the advert...

Hello? Is this not a good time?

I don't understand. Sometimes this bit of floor is warm then a few hours later it's cold. I think there's a problem with your central heating.

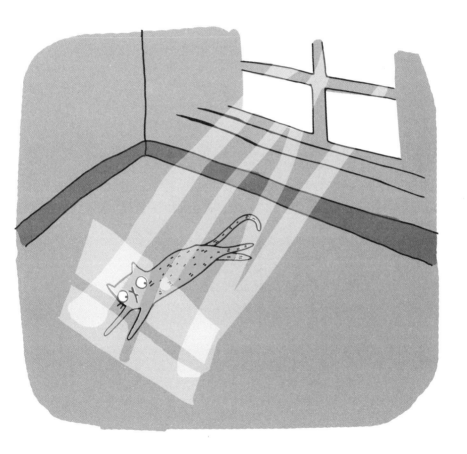

In all honesty? Not your best angle.

Have I mentioned how much
I love you?

Hello?

Fine. I hate you anyway.

I have literally no idea who you are.

This bed is amazing – and it smells incredible.

Your tap is broken. I'm doing my best to save the water but you should probably call a plumber.

Honestly. This place would fall apart without me.

A step too far.

Next door's cat was here. As usual,
you were nowhere to be found.

I'll be down in a couple of years.

One more bowl of that revolting
tuna mulch and I'll be 'missing' too.

Seriously – what is going on?
I'm freezing over here.

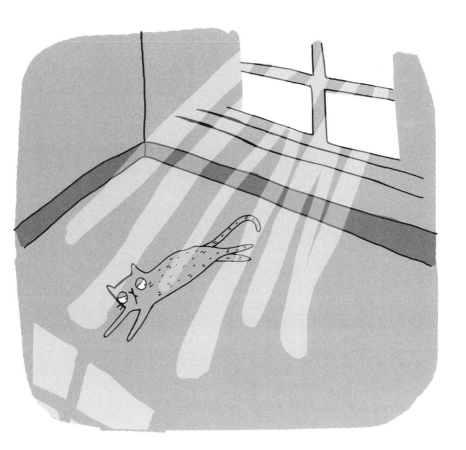

Why can't you see the value
of my presents?

.

It's either him or me.

The best day ever. You're so warm …
and for once you're keeping quiet…
Why can't it always be like this?

Stop it. Just stop it. Even I'm sick of Instagram cats.

There's still something not right about this wall... Why aren't you doing anything?

I'm leaving you for the neighbour.

It's not you, it's the prawns and cream at number 52.